Talisman
A Novel of Amnesia

****

Jolaoso Prettythunder

PRICKLY PEAR PUBLISHING

Acknowledgements

Talisman
A Novel of Amnesia

ISBN: 978-1-889568-17-1
Library of Congress Control Number: 2022948501
First Edition, 2023
Published by Prickly Pear Publishing
in the United States of America
www.pricklypearpublishing.com

Some of these poems have appeared in Poets Responding, Love and Prayers for Fukushima, Poetry Bay, Cloud Women's Quarterly Journal, and Community of Writer's Café.

Author's note: The people in this book are all beings from my imagination and any resemblance to persons living or dead is purely coincidental.

Cover art design Prickly Pear Publishing
Cover photography courtesy of the author

10 9 8 7 6 5 4 3 2 1

"The here and the beyond are enough, but there were a few angels for whom it was not enough: who demanded a third dimension--who sought fusions, communes, who ate each other and created sex."

— Dale Pendell from Pharmako/Poeia: Plant Powers, Poisons, and Herbcraft

In loving memory of my beloved husband,
Iluminado Maldonado Ifagbemi Ogbetumako

Talisman
A Novel of Amnesia

Contents

Prelude- Mama Iris

i have never been pretty
something you would want
to look at for long
in marketplaces trading posts and bazaars
i have made old men cough
children squint
and their aunties made them
wear their clothes inside out and backwards
after i touched their eggs and cork bottles
i got sick once and they called
for the blind healer
they will remember none of this
only my harsh tongue
and how I wouldn't love them
and think thoughts they think correct
they lower their voices
and give me drugs
not close enough to opium
to make me forget
to extinguish me
i laugh for a long time
they come undone
as i drift off they are still
trying to book passage
into my bruised and cracked mind

they want to chart this
become geologists of madness
i laugh the grapes from the vine
i laugh and sound like cigarettes and
        whiskey hoarse
i dream of horses
riding fast
not looking behind me
i can see them with the eye
on the back of my head

Chapter 1- Prophecy

Those dark lilies outside the cold window
the widow's peak rising up in the shadow
how did they come to be here
        she asks   Whispers
looking down at the black lilies
        beneath the pines
the children did not know
        shouldn't have looked   touching
into that Stellar Jay's nest
she tore into her babies that summer
from the cold window always watching
he stood

Chapter 2- Railway Vision

Fox in the chicken coop
        We run across the field
The boy smells like sun and late wind
        I sleep soundly
when you hold me and when I sing
        to the stars they get brighter
Fox in the chicken coop

Chapter 3- Which You Must Swim To

We take the apples from the old man's tree and don't feel bad
because he never eats them anyway We fall down and tumble
through the neighbor's orchard That's the same day Lynnea fell
into the nettles from the rope swing Later out at Dungeness we eat raw
oysters from the shore Turning over grey rocks the color of November
high fever showed me the spotted dancers

Chapter Red- To be sung in Winter

Small Serpent   Winged
        Here are your antlers
        wrapped in thunder

Mother Trucker- The Chapter of Question

The young girl hikes up her skirt   Shows her
        skinned knees to her uncle
They say I'm cold for saying this   I'm still
        thinking about that girl   I say it's dirt
There's incest and penetration in the air
        The galvanized roof   His Formica table
Her Johnnie Walker   It's been decades and
        still she thinks her daughter is 9

Blessed Chapter

Not just in a Blue Moon   we made love
        secretly in Côte d'Ivoire
It does not matter what you use it for
        just a little time left
Wrap me around lilies
I am the field
cane harvest
a scrapped sky
See how I fade with the hours
                                        years
                                    glances
                                        words
this is my palm   map
of a way
some say

Intravenous Chapter- The Day Moon

Cuss me
shut the windows first
unplug the guest house fan
we can sweat this out
in malaria land
cerebral they say
can't you see it coiled up with my liver?
it has found its way around the booze and
now rests deep within the cerebral matter
lying contently in the back of my head
i am delirious
a woman dead
a child still waiting

Robe of Fern-
Chapter of Disappearing

i once was somebody's pretty
wore neroli and rose absolute
season of pearls and cashmere
cinnamon in the brandy
crumbling under his touch
fingers between my legs i quivered
wanted more
sweeter than honey spun baklava
i believed
the sun went down in October
by late winter i was a heathen
the winds howled sounded like war
i could relate
now I walk the streets of Chinatown
and try to kick the mean reds
the ocean pulls back and it is too far
to wade in the water
i sit on granite and line up bullwhip
circular stones
waterlogged feather for a flag
my home
i forget my tongues
tossing the family name into the fire pit
–moving on

forked lightning
there is sacrifice in the ferns
where lacking wings i crawl
he wanted to meet the whore in me
then make her disappear me disappear
goodbye
'til I am at the kitchen table looking at grocery
ads
no wonder i will leave you
driving through

Your Palm Read in Late April-
Chapter of Self

It's true It's not a seasonal thing It is
ongoing and will not pass A maiming
thing
that has us collide take pills smoke various
medicines stay drunk collect and
dispose of lovers lose small pieces of paper
Horrible you think how it would be
to just drive your fucking car off highway 1
straight into the ocean Ravenous
you go to Chinatown buy roast duck and rice
Eat the whole thing in your room with
your hands glad you're alone
happy to not share

Chapter 10- Which You Read in Fever

Lilacs bloom outside the window   Here
        the alligator and water moccasin
        is your brother
You bathe in verbena hibiscus and horsetail
        color the water with bluing in the
outside
tub beneath the old cypress   You keep
        the letters   You feel you've put enough
miles down

Long Chapter

They stay up past 3:00 am behind the
painted door   called each other
'Liar'
destroyed it all

Chapter Ecstasy

They hated each other for it
hunger
need
lost sleep and   don't be so tender

Chapter God

On her knees she forges for the root
Mary is a flamenco dancer   our holy mother
you give permission
                offerings
one small bowl of oranges
baguettes for the boys on the corner
a small leather bag

Thief Chapter- Chapter of Angels

I have underestimated August
half-sister to the moon that kills
Battle Mountain Nevada–
town of masturbation and
        Pabst Blue Ribbon beer
good for only one thing
to catch a train out of hell
you thought it was love
until you realized you hadn't
        written in months
she had just about murdered your muse
you saw this one night when you stayed
        up and chain smoked
drinking the rest of the booze in the house
the sex was good but now left you
        Unsatiated
plastic bags caught on a cyclone fence
this place of exhaustion
desolation
night comes

Night Chapter- Prayer at Devil's Gulch for the Disremembered

Tonight dogs worry their chains
she can still smell the raw cold
        steel of the gun barrel
the cherry grip handle   Crosshatched
        Well oiled
tonight she tosses cedar sweetgrass and
        tobacco
        into to the rubbish bin
forsaking all protection
the acrid taste of a backhand

                                        copper
                                rises in her mouth
                                  brings her home
to
calloused hands   edge of the woods   unseen
where furled leaves turn black
        when no one sees
beneath the weight

Chapter 16- What the Wind Knows

dirt wind
cave wind
5 and clown wind
Eagle Soldier
how I crave you
especially in May
my circle of stones
my long ride home
thunder above Fist Mountain

Chapter 17- Day of the Dogstar

do not become acquainted with her
she will only make you question your ideas
of what beauty and ugliness is
you will wish later that she had spared you
    the details
and instead looked up   to the sky
closed her mouth
smell of rain
Maidenhair fern   a beauty down deep
pocketful of lichen
wishing rocks under the redwoods
you will want to dig
find a reason
it gets in between the cracks
    a crack
has gone too deep
passed the gag reflex and has become
    too easy now
no ceremony can wash you clean   sweep it
    all away
your mind goes to the gutter
    so very easily now
leave it alone
you can't save her

Dirty Secret- Chapter of Barbed Wire

he found her in dream
on knees
digging
his face showed the wars he had fought in
Survived
death is never pretty

her face a pool of water
showed other things
where she sat up
nights in song
nights of crawling
where god didn't go
over arrowheads   over Jack Daniel's semen
over Fist Mountain

Pussy Money- Chapter of Loss

the serenity of youu embrace dropped off
the edge of the West Coast
haven't seen it since
i was a fool then
thought you were my strength
no one could tell me otherwise back then
dumb and beautiful
i didn't wake up until i lost everything
crawled around the bedroom floor
smelling your work shirts saving
your letters
dining on valium vodka and air
i became a skeleton
my own fault
rebuilt my life from coupons pussy money
Medical and Christmas gifts
from Adopt-a-Family
the mean cashier lined up my food stamps
on the produce scale
called on the intercom for assistance
"Food Stamp assistance on check stand 4,
food Stamp assistance on check stand 4"
i called her a bitch to her face and meant it
when i was on the ground
so many women were thrilled

i see them from time to time
they haven't aged well

Chapter of Angels

Dear You

The seasons sometimes seem too long because I am unable to touch you This fog and coolness come in and create a forced examination and deconstruction of night There is excess in my longing and I hunger for your mouth in a way no one should crave another

–Me

Chapter 21- Moon of Soldiers and Priests

back rooms and alleyways
see me behind the dumpster
dirty flower bending over

Emerald Chapter- Human Animal

Beg for amnesia
it has come to this
you woke up today and know with certainty
        that there are vacancies
in your last year of college and the day
        you moved into that crappy apartment
in that season of sunflowers the year
        you drove through Joshua Tree and
the time you chose the attractive beautiful
        lover over the sweet one
who adored you you regret it and
        like magic no one knows
like a trick or a gift perhaps you were born
        with this ability to die inside
slowly smiling your lover spouse co-
        workers cousins brothers sisters
even the dirt and moon find you to be present
        but you are more
than countries away

It would require months of preparation and
        contraband in trade
to reach you now then the vaccines and
        a special diet:

the emerald around the sunset
glass from the collision
diamonds collected by crippled children
the poison ring
you've seen too much

Queen Chapter- Where You
Will Have to Blame Everyone

For a Chola who thought I grew up privileged

she said she was from cement
and that I was from the trees
that I wasn't like her
called me elite   entitled   proud   ignorant
        to the struggle
that i needed to learn respect and didn't know
        how hard it all was
this was a mistake
she had heard my songs and laughter
        from the Mesa
took notice of my small gourds filled
        with chaparral   piñon   juniper
said my view of the world was different
thought me too sheltered   too precious
failed to see my one-way ticket out of hell
my seasons of exile and crawling
where i ate Fels Naptha soap for lunch
a backhand for dinner
season of the gun
a time to collect keloids and cancer
where you have to get on your hands and
        knees   to get right
wear an armor of Coors pull tabs sip jello

through a wired jaw
lose faith in jesus while eating your Cheerios
in a bowl of water
i won't go back
and i say with my mouth— you are
an eight-year-old at 65
i say outright you haven't worked
on your shit
and you're right
i am not like you

Chapter 24- A Place of Longing

he enters her thoughts
makes her whisper
she calls him by his true name
remembering thunder
                    c'est trop
like the scent of seashells and spikenard
combined with woodsmoke and whisky
a howl   a heaving
a kind of grief
strange power
that hangs the moon each night

February- Chapter of Hibernation

here the grass shakes and hisses
a song there   a remembering
small lynx is a wave in the meadow
you'll miss her me if you're not looking
she turns from the ugly
that precedes some people
waves them on   keep moving   smells bad
she is lowly here
place of dirt and the long gaze
singing a traveling song
she gathers the waste
dancing counter clockwise
until the dead are honored
she is 7000 swallows turned from a butterfly
burlap sack for a dress
shotgun shells   mezcal and
          Sphaeralcea ambigua
are her medicines
she cusses and makes all this up
it's late she's still up
hasn't blinked yet
see her
the dreamer elk
disappear
become fog

Chapter 26- Twin Dragon

A Fishturn Poem

They whispered behind the closed door
        some say they were angels   some say
demons   because of the way they floated
        on clouds   they eventually shape
shifted from dirt   from the filth   mouth full
        of lies   sting of the bird pepper   and
1000 gutted perch   transformed first into
        Phoenix   then he into the
mountain   her the sea   oftentimes
        they can be heard
not seen   he a pack of wolves she
the descending sound of the canyon wren

She's Gone Again- Stillborn Chapter

where i vomit
a lie
out onto the pavement
inside that brick building is the club
          where i danced
and hated-loved it
orange and red
cyan and black
season of fucking the too young Jew boy and
          the too rough Arab
who actually almost killed me   yet i told
          no one
a stupid season
a dumb time
the rain brought autumn and she
          was stillborn
so i stayed on the couch until winter
then danced for the sad men
wore dead fox
pockets full
pussy money
smeared lipstick
i was cheap with expensive boots
then drove to truck stops
to eat pancakes

sip Nescafé

she was a normal girl
she knew lilacs and roses
she sang with her feet
in the bayou

season of perfume from the duty free
season of phone cards and contraband
a time to keep the Xanax on a keychain
make copies of the passport chronicle
the disaster
take names
lose people

Chapter 28- Where You Whisper Walk

Twilight
nasturtiums monkshood and one datura
        blossom in the outdoor bath here opium
floats in our tea   we are eating warm
        bread from the Jew baker   wild
boar sausage and smoking cigars after
midnight   driftwood smoke tangled in our
hair   always   one night when no one was
        there we briefly swam naked with the
phosphorescents traced mountain lion
        tracks with our tongues at sunrise

Chariot

Can I carry on like 500 convicts 25 to Life
colder than ice colder
strap me down
how many men does it take
"You are vulgar," they tell me
requiem from the rivers
sweet overflow
dread washed in the sea
aloes and shea couldn't ever soften his edges
they took away my husband in chains
he used to bring me flowers that I swear
were funeral arrangements
perfume of camphor and
formaldehyde
he waited too long for me to die
i outlived him
barely
slammed and tossed
i was free falling
he tried so hard to be a felon
a thousand times over
he succeeded
vandalizing my interior first
with steady hands
moving like an executioner

he was so precise
kept calling for the guillotine
to roll my head
i wasted away
the antique band vowed
enslaved me
it hung around my finger wrist
then my neck
i stepped out of it one day
they named me feral
said my prayers won't reach God
many said he was so humble
but I saw how he was
always so hungry
insatiable
        he got off easy

Temple- Chapter of Silence

the lunar moth
at the near mouth
of the bay
blue butterfly
in the night
navigate
at the moss gate
press our face
close
this deep loam
so cool on each side
of the hour
we
who dream
call them by name
who is contrary?
sees
the rearranged
vegetation
steeple of trees
slant of the hills
        moving

Chapter Vagabond-
Ritual Confession

where i lost
my house   my job   my mind   my people
moon of suicide attempts and
        activated charcoal
Christmas of 5150s and restraints
discharged from the Phoenix Ward
i stared at walls   Lived on a couch
        Lined up pills
Drank cheap wine and hired a babysitter
        to be mom
for my kids   the shower was much too long
        of a walk
i stayed put   sleeping through the seasons
then ran away to Paris
happy to be a wretch
sucking my lovers cock in the alleyways
        of Place de Clichy
i stayed drunk until noon   Hoped he'd go
        back to his wife
reckless   i called him bad names
        flirted with his brother
bought shoes and perfume then lost them
        Lost me
my ability to navigate between

dream and myth
day or night had vanished
mouthful of Xanax to stifle the screams
later i was found floating spinning on a leaf
in a creek
delirious for many winters i consumed
tule fog and Nescafé
for breakfast lunch and dinner
i'm careful with my words and deeds now
collect indigo stars lichen
see me beneath the madrone clamoring
animal drivel i whisper into the pines
where i make a strange ceremony
and am laria
am mycelium

In Her Hometown- Her Chapter

Three legged dogs roam the streets out here
dirt poor and lying   she runs
        an extension cord from her trailer
to theirs and watches the local news
        eats pot pies from the frozen aisle
she knows where love is   it's easier this way

Warriors- Chapter of Lightning and Thunder, an Honor Song

Not made but born he said   sent her 4
          campaign flags and rubies from Iraq
warhorse who never came home   God
          wears a Green Beret
let's honor him

Chapter 34- Where you Burn your Garbage

the people i might need to tell
are far and away
this is how you can reach them
in the night morning really
between 2 and 4am
sshh be silent
take into account the season
and how the moon hangs
then send out the calling
offering these things

1. one six pack of Guinness
2. a bottle of rum
3. Spanish thyme from Jemma's yard
4. 6 ounces of smoked fish
5. 2 sprays of Versace's "The Dreamer"
6. a bag of water
7. the will to live
8. the ability to crawl
9. the song whispered in our ear on the Mourning Ground

you wonder how you ever returned
you wonder if you ever did

Matriarchy

My mother's womb was a sandbox
        Sandbox as in war of the desert
We tossed the family name into the pit
        On our way to buy a pickle
from the corner store

Switchback- Riding the Long Night

An Ode to PTSD

with might holy
hold and grip her belly
protecting
like a life or contraband within
shudder and tremble
in the damp night
twitch and shiver
like the dark-wet
hide of the equine
tight
muscle of the mind
that little chaos
and no washboard
can push it under
can you get with that
get with this
you want an acronym
you wanna try this
you wanna
you wanna
break this down
she wants to break it down too
like a hookah
or a syringe
or a gun

handle it
inured to the coal dark
and the sentinels have bowed out
there will be no negotiations
it is always drastic
nights like this
come down like a cleaver
before stainless steel was ever made

Summer- Chapter of Sex ~ When Soldiers Come Home

i give you
ebb and flood
fistfuls of harvest at the junction
of seasons
lark in the tangled meadow shows
your eyes hands
a ridge gullies
our bodies are painted
we are ashborn
and are returning
back to magma
back to stars
i will rest here
and am close
dove sunset
a song there
dreaming

Chapter 38- Caravel

Wherever you leave my
hollow bones   jackal and
hyena will know my name
twine my hair   shadow the
sun   sing your lullaby
of sweet lament
set sail in your caravel
on a bed of cypress and vetiver
speak of me as you would
the night heron and phosphorescents
in the hidden cove
and the powdered sandalwood
rubbed into your palms

Effulgence

call of the angels
turn of the colors
turn to stone
it's in the thunder
shudder of the earth
gathering of the souls
in a field is a cold truth
upon the ground of Gabriel
i am hope's daughter
and i bound towards
the song at sunrise

Chapter 40- The Last Supper ~ The Secret Chapters

Smoked goat mango bats hot peppers
and large grubs   fed to me
food of the Gods   i didn't have to be told
i consumed them knowingly   sopped up
the sauces and left nothing for the flies
swarming about the compound
that was another part of Africa but later
in the North among votive prayer
and women who look through eyes
          that have witnessed
the Far-off   their genitals having been
          carefully sliced
off with a freshly broken coke bottle
in a tent   in the desert i am told to eat
a small thick slice triangular in shape
cooked in camel's milk fired by camel dung
prepared slowly covered by a burlap sac
"...eat," i am urged
it is strangely delicious
i know better than to ask   and without
doing so   i am told the source of the oddly
textured dense yet tender meat
"It is for you because you are here. For you,"
they say   I look into the eyes of a young boy

he is too young to be silent
raising his hand without hesitation
"It is this, the most center part,
        the palm of man"

Rio Nido II

fernwise she can hear your true song
and remembers too much
shape shifting woman
that turns into white water
a cauldron of raptors
a salamander under the stone
she wears winter's lichen for a coat
deer hoof bells   her crown
and draws lightning out
on a madrone leaf   using a piece of coal
stopping the rain from time to time
using dry earth as medicine
          wrapped in a charm
axe hitting hardwood
year round
it is the season of hibernation
always
there is a whispering
that can be heard you know
a turning away from the main road
we gather the dew from the fern
draw in the loam
bottle it
trillium ovatum
pedicularis densiflora

whisper walking under the veil

The Empty Dress

she leaves it at the bottom of the closet
too sentimental to toss it
piling shoes and boxes of old poetry over it
it won't go away
make it go away
failed marriage broken vows and it's not all
his fault
she learned lessons in those chapters
maybe
learned how she wasn't always right
too proud
walking out of the house after midnight
barefoot along the highway
crazy or something close to it
wanted to prove some kinda something
he never followed
in fact didn't even know she'd left
sleeping soundly content
badger slinked low in the bush
no one cared
years later
she sacrificed her own self
again
gave everything away
quit the big job

left her friends and family
flew thousands of miles to meet
        her new lover
no amount of fucking was enough
he never saw her magic
season of blindness
again
returning home
alone

The Desert Remembers Me ~ Peyote Chapter

and how I lay with the sidewinders
  S s s s s
cave dweller
and i gather the waste
  S s s s s
dreaming with the holiest of men's society
i am actually a bad woman
  S s s s s
singing man songs when no one is listening
  S s s s s s
folded sky are you my relation?
forked lightning i know you are

Love is an Aroma

that I couldn't get rid of
aired out the house
lit candles
Worked spells
Walked outside and
hollered for my own self
from the front door
an echo
nothing came back
i was gone
a skeleton
had been since the bad winter
waited nights for that call
Knew it wouldn't come Still waited
desperate and absurd I was still up
at 3:00 AM looking so beautiful
just in case
perfect hair and buttery skin For no one
Not even myself   now i am intimate
            with the horizon
With Clouds With the trickle of the stream
Know them well
Am the fifth wind
a sideways glance
a lost itinerary

hating weekends
where i imagine my used to be lover
          fucking the new one
a wretch (yes me)
i grew bad claws Dug into the dirt
To conjure To hide To Die
So stupid
learned late   how magic can be lost

Lover- Chapter of Knowing

you my love
you are the reason the swallows
come together part then reunite
your palms mark every moonrise
        of our eternal union
your eyes witness and contain water
        from every sea
you have known me on every shore
        in all realms
twilight originates from your exhale
the lightning flash is you seeking me out
        in a dark season
come to me always
peonies blossom within you and are
        my song at dusk
i love you beyond distance
the tule fog arrives quickly when i grow
        silent at missing your touch
your lips a topo map that leads
        to my inner longings
you are my glow   my true essence
        in and around me
the somniferum weeps her medicine
at your presence in the garden
your poetry frames the morning star

our love making a monsoon
that heals the grief of all lovers
dew appears when i think of you
1000 may birds soar and circle
when your name is invoked
you are the mountain
the stone that remembers it all

First Light- Farm Chapter

4am
she lays in the hay
too cold to move
she keeps her fire inside
hums then sings an honor song to her lover
on the other side of the hour
he catches it on the west wind

Chapter 47- Kaleidoscope

It is getting close

Too close to February
A month that wants to knock the hell
out of me
See my face swell up my jaw rearranged
I will be able to view the world
with one eye

The contusions will circle a secret
color wheel
Reserved for those who meet with collision

1 Red
2 Strange magenta
3 Purple
4 Black
5 Sickly yellow
6 Invisible spider web

A face that is better hidden

That
Silences men

And causes odd delight in some women
Who can't help but whisper to each other
"She had it coming"
they hope I will scar

I am laughing at them

If only they could see
how I have crawled
trying to reach the sea breeze
From the iron bed
To the veranda
Like a dog

I can even bark when fucked don't
        they know this?
Then magically the following morning
        with a baby on my back

1 Set afternoon tea
2 Take a cutlass to the yard
3 Tote water
4 Smile when told to
5 Rely on lucky charms
6 Play pretend

Years later faint scars will be visible
        under direct sunlight

One eye extraordinarily skewed
A permanent hematoma for life
It is my beautiful red jewel
Outlandish intimate bond
Secret vow

Catalyst to my new lover:
Papaver somniferum

lunar moth
goodnight
black
black
black

Holyhand

I am saying datura grows in colonies
on abandoned roads on the hips
        of the interstate
i do don't remember what she says
lost several hours days even
ghost rattle
I am saying the dumb sky above looked down
on my galvanized roof   my castle
        and two bucks locked antlers
In front of the house
03:00 am
dragging each other 150 feet
I call the dream helper by name
It's that time again
dirt
ash
mist captured
The women of my clan tossed the family
        name into the pit
I too burn the bridges
Goodbye
My vision can change with the invisible
        borders that
I see   then cross
Trespassing

Yet further
I push it reach the edges some kind of
        darkness that brightens
Don't look in the skeleton closet
        you will find me there
The town dump   ocean   ravine last stand
        of redwoods
I am the rubbish of the compound
Being eaten by the village chickens
I shapeshift into the sailor a crossroads
Then the common wife the storm flower
perfect whore your queen
I am on the porch tethered to a cinder
        block that lays in the crabgrass
This is exile self-chosen
I nap in the sun
Irresponsible
Drawing it out with a stick in the dirt
I am the green hoop around the sun
on far away days
I see you in your manner
I speak in your Way
Dressing the house in tea and cakes
Spirit plates left for the dead
I know the songs for war love
invisibility and undoing the sorcery
I tie knots in the rhythm
I say outright you have abandoned

your own self
I say to you those matching dishes
and pillows is your spirit
malnourished   That formal garden the same
I speak that I fear my own black magic
and what I can do
what I have already done
I say I know these trees and which way
to glance
to accomplish it all
Blood in the hollow
1 2 3 4 5 6 7
This is what I am saying
This is the language I speak

Angels and Demons

you are
the phosphorescence
my leaf
my wing
lunar moth
sweet in my mouth
as Doug fir tips
a taste I know well
flood tide combined with ash
i seek you always
on the singed wings of angels
on the moist tongue
furled in dreams
i lay down in the loam
with Michael
with Gabriel
who are assigned
to the cardinal directions
of your astral body
i hear you on the empty sea
immense tide
mouth of the river
i stand on this coastal shore naked
holding Thunderstones
beneath the tyrant sky

my unbraided hair
this temple of birds
hallucination
earth and sky
day and night
calling out
in the other way

Deeply Mary- Chapter Lichen

chase her through the dead pine
draped in her robe of nettle– pine pitch
she pulls the ceanothus from deep below
"those hips are too beautiful for these
        backwoods" say the boys
they want to unbraid her breed her
ceanothus bleeds blood red
fortitude
patience
marks this ally
hands like shovels she can coax it's medicine
        to the surface
"Mary, Mary" the boys call to the five winds
they want to mount her from behind
hard
give it to her
in ways forbidden
bury it in her
they want to break all the taboos
she wears the war paint to greet
the skinwalkers who lose interest
        when they meet her
belly to the loam feral
their eyes leave holes in hollow logs
        but do not touch her

disappearing quietly back
        to the shadow places
coyote is laughing at them
somehow he too loves her so much
her red lips are hard to handle
allied to the medicine of the ceanothus
she is too fierce to be woman
perhaps they can bypass her contrary nature
just skim over the little bit of thunder
reach into her bundle
perhaps

The Fifth Wind

I am the fifth wind
i am here here and here
ebb tide
dark moon
i pull the roots down deeper
yank with my teeth
hunt down sickness in its hiding place
stop lying
i will level the village
wearing fire for a skirt
i bathe in the dust
dancing counterclockwise
don't follow me where i go
you The Dead cannot trouble me
for i am the blue deer
and can capture all your medicine
from my mouth comes the fog
fernborn
lighting born
i gather the waste and remove it
yerba Santa and Grindilia combined
is my Medicine

Medicine Woman

because i know the name of monsters
am a monster
hands like shovels
whip tailed
can coax the medicine from the root
rhizome of sleep
rhizome of twitching and perspiration
making them diaphoretic
making them joyful
deer arms
making poison
making the cure
destroying it all
in one night

Night Train at Luster Gap

Where I waited for you
Having taken the last train into
        Cheyenne Wyoming
I'm in my half-priced red dress 1:45am
        In a cheap motel
I am perfectly groomed Silk stockings
        A garter belt
Eyebrows lips hair so detailed
Between my legs I am washing
        with orange blossom water and vanilla
I am the perfect lover
Bucket of ice on the nightstand
Laying still on this bed Legs smooth
        from my Bic razor
I love-hate my need for you
And hope your wife will just go away
Absurd in the dark I rearrange
        the way my hair falls on the pillow
Like the dead really And my hands
        are like ice
A wreck and too proud to admit
        the fool I am
Having used every last penny I had
On this ticket bottle of wine
oil that you will smell and think me magic

Irresistible   See how easily I make you laugh
I know you and what you want
Snakes are in my belly And I know it
My cuticles bleed where I cannot stop
        picking at them
I am a fraud and have no intention of
Allowing you to see this
Perfect I lay on these dirty sheets
        In this cheap motel
Getting up 25, 200, 250 times to peep
        out the window
Pour more orange blossom between my legs
        Apply more lipstick
Dawn – You never come
Circles under my eyes ridiculous
        mouth so dry
        preposterous with red lipstick
I smell sour I am alone With
        a stupid bucket of water by the bed
Find a corner of the room to call
        my own and fuck myself
To the sound of the infomercial
I did too much
I do too much
I can never make this right

Massembo

For Yaya Clementine

The smell
of burnt garbage and war
the compound of tires and galvanize
        piles of brick
rusted nails   Tossed out batteries
a thin fabric blows in the doorway
you're seeing – then not seeing
a slight breeze rules this
chickens peck through the rubbish heap
eating what chicken won't
who knows this place?
not so far away

in the pot is a chicken
so lean you have to suck the bones
find marrow and mix it
with your own saliva and blood
sustain yourself on your own will to live

How did all these tin bowls from China
        get here?

wild dogs are running
they soon will be in the pot

you are left to sort out hair cartilage
bone and the sharp jaws of fruit bats
teeth so intricate and amazing
that in your delirium you examine them
your tongue a fine tool to find protein
you will live

Ground Drawings

Because you once knew a woman
Who kept rum of the scorpion
In one bottle and the holy water
From the Jesuits in another
They sat side by side in
The Dove room
Apothecary of the Worlds
When she died she
Gifted these bottles to you
The water was to cool your head
The rum to keep you alive on
The far-off shore where you
Go to seek her
At the three-way you bottle
Her footprints under the tree below
The offerings and use it to bathe yourself
In this way you will come to know her
And know why they could not ride small
Horses

Chapter 56- White of Her Eye

You will not find me on that shore
in the groves of Cypress you knew me
        to be kin to
My tracks themselves have changed
This blood does not run in the way
        you remember
And you will not recognize my scent
Your memories are so old Tall Ghost
lost solider
haggard night
one who whored the drum
Here is my mouth
Opening in a way you never knew
Breathing hot as I work the Ceanothus
Four hours in just her and I
Her roots bleed blood red
        she gives me a good fight
Eventually coming out in one piece
You once froze me and
I grew cold
So cold that touching the fir tips
        made them whither
And if you looked close
        you could see the sclera
Circle below the brown of my iris as

I looked toward the Farlons
Floating iris
A sure sign that I would die
a sudden and tragic death
But my eyes shape shifted
And I am no longer a skeleton
15:00
she cursed the morning star
the page was blank
she drove and drove
On the ridge
The dreamer elk walks the tule fog
Disappears
Today
Metal hitting wood
I am chopping the old timber for
the Moon When the Babies Cry
And am too far north
for you ever to be here

This skin holds me just

True Dragon- Chapter Insomnia

A Fishturn poem

It is way past 3AM
I know you know I saw you pass
        them iron tracks
Your Jack Daniels
Your Lucky Strikes
Your "Leave Me Alone" ways
Thinking about your Dirty Mama
        thinking about your Boy Blue
You have come to rest your head
        upon my torso
Telling me it's late... too late
        for Indian Summer
And that somehow you have lost a season
        possibly several

The season when some dry flowers
Pack fruit in jars   comfort for that
        cold bitch February?

February
Moon of dimensional smuggling place
        of echoes and shape shifters
Season of Broken Rosary

That chokes asphyxiates
It will come you know sooner
        than we realize
Red lipstick smeared sheets
        extra shoe polish
Polished grip of the gun handmade
        expertly crafted
Angora wool silk We'll wear robes
        of small prey
And draw with a stick in the dirt
Our mouths meet in a confusion of Raspberry
        Vanilla and Xanax

Season of
Scotch and bourbon a time to stay behind
        smoke   forget
And you close the bar
Absolute of Cèpes Costus and Black Spruce
Define and guard the nights
Cannabis takes a back seat to the Shadows
        it simply won't do
We have laid down in the Night Garden
                cronophagoi
                distant nuncio
                    lost days

I call upon Labdanum and Blond Tobacco
        and need fire

Michael
Gabriel
Raphael

To balance the cloying and sickening
sweetness of too much floral
Too much treble the bright lights
and paranoia
Overindulgence and insomnia

Bitch Season
She wants to see me dead you know
It's ok
We know death well
humans born to kill

Like hyena like lion like bear
Sometimes we eat our own

I am drinking each day by 10:00
Beautiful dinners leather coats
the newest shoe/boot
The vitamins herbs roots One tablespoon
of dragon bones in grain
Pure water enough fiber

I too want to tell lies
And leave the garbage bill water bill
        and Lovers
To pile up
Fruit, cheese- all sustenance
Left to rot
Make it go away
All go away
For I have gone

See me without my beauty lace shoved
        in my mouth to stifle the screams
I want only to kiss to kiss
Sex is so overrated absurd and desperate
Bad for my state of mind
I will Tango when I am well
                    hold both your hands
                        look into your eyes
                                15:00
                            finally falling

This is penetration

        Please
Do not speak
For sometimes I have confused the monster
        with the man you see

But don't be deceived don't take
          my silence for frailty

I know enough to come out of this alive
To get up and walk 100 feet from the house
And call the Dream Helper by name

Chapter 58- Westwind

Scarlet star
Heyoka His Medicine
she is wearing
a headdress of matchsticks
robe of dog skins

Her small feet are toughened
        to the bad bones
as she walks across the backs of men with her
black lonesome thoughts
on roads too tough to hoe

She is counting small bills in the shade
because there is still a small pride
washing her hands thoroughly in the dirt

She counts her money and
        will hold her head up
and no one will know she came from trash
because she keeps her nails clean
whites of eyes clear

West wind
indifferent
blooms in the night

unlucky then lucky

There are swallows in the sky here

She is unbraiding her hair which drags
        in the gully
and wherever she passes
        the wood will not catch

Hollering Madrone

Back behind the
Hollering Madrone

Where
sting by sting the berry
and ghost pine
tight the sinew four weave
holy rosary draped upon my torso

Where
scraped and pushed into the dirt
                    and it did know me

another grave
another death
crust or loam
the terra firma
granite sand
foraminifera
ground down to
silica and chalk

So we take the opportunity to look deeply
chert the arrow
through the obsidian eye

and leave it
in the sawgrass
for tomorrow's finder

There are woman like this
who can claw their way
without a shovel
can push with their hands
or
tug lightly

The hollering Madrone
is screaming and will not
burn for you

Creator
I am your child
can sing the Mariner's Song
or the wail of the desert and prairie

Along the bays or mesas
cradle Pangaea without faltering

Scoop
of the mussels
bite
of the barnacle
whip

of the cold scoop
fierce overnight cage bloom
of the dune primrose
pressed between the psalms
or rubbed
into the compass smoke
toward the God Door

Gray Blanket

Quiet thicket
canopy of wood
some become sleepy
some will roam
some stand very still
still dreaming
look
gaze into a water
firmament
in the crux
of long shadows
the stick indian
is in
the here
I have been singing so long
I sing this song now
dream out that
that
I am saying
upon the gray blanket
I shook them snakes
one became twenty
I shook them off
ten
I shook them off
they are gone now

and won't return
peace returned
they say make a song
I am singing
to remember
and sing it

in the new places entering
we do that now

Across Bog Bridge- Chapter of Honey

Come to your dirty mamma
i am your Violetta
that you look for
in the half light
and am wet and dripping
with the canal camps
muddy
My toes grip
the red root of the
black willow
which call the honeybees
beeswax seals my lips
and I say nothing of how you come to me
in the quiet
in the chaos
I woke up naked
cool
with only your
new moon murmurs
and fireflies to clothe me
shake me
and jingle
my buckeye and catskins
perhaps I'll be lucky tomorrow
I'm here with a

low down sorry man
He comes around
when my pockets are full
we eat catfish and
the corn we catch it with
drink corn whiskey or rye
he likes my one red dress
how it snags on the Formica table
and eats from granny's pie plates
licking them clean with his tongue
there are bones stacked high
          on old newsprint
on the packed earthen floor
I am being scolded again
"You can't even carry a conversation
but your camelback shack
is filled with verse and broken pottery
and you sing with the uncaged birds that
flock to your veranda
cussing me in your languages
how do you carry on?"
you have already disappeared
and it makes some sound
crazy when they say they've seen
you walk pass the petrol
stand at night
why not just stay in your swamp?"
I found a clutch from that

black rat snake
I've been watching her
and know some who taste the air like that
I'm singing
watching her tongue
someone is still scolding scolding
talking talking
it sounds like
wood ducks
somewhere in all this
I hear the Bloodroot's pitch
calling from the holler
that red dress pales
against its medicine in the jug
sitting in the veranda

Red Delta Topography

You have come here
beneath the still leaf
petal
metal against bone
the stench of embargo
barbed wire broken bottles atop
        cement walls
too much gardenia or the sickly smell
of confined jasmine which weeps
once cut from the vine
you are my familiar
lone nightingale
hear the festivities or the wail of funeral time
let us hush in the temple and laugh
        in the corridors
pushed against the pillars unfastened
        in the groves
we have lost our reference points and
        time zones
were insignificant
unless we are applying
the neroli and lavender oils
to the pounding pounding
the earth is shaking
kaleidoscope migraine

of timeshift to our temples
this is what you get
when you cross too much water
in one lifetime
floating
floating
                    I think I have drowned
you have lost something somewhere
between this border and one erased
smeared away
as in the soft charcoal drawings
the place between a woman's legs
where men get lost
color of musk oil
male deer
blood red
contraband
ambergris
in the hidden containers
of enormous ships and
on tiny airstrips
come even closer
it is dangerous
like stolen honey
oil of hashish
to fall into and over again and again
I have breathed in enough cedar
        and sandalwood

over these long nights and miles that my
sweat falls into beads onto the myrrh
I am stringing them into a collar

A royal thing
braid me into your stoic nodding as you
pass the men at market silently
praying or cussing
bind me into the copper that fills your mouth
as if you got hit
very hard in the face
swallow me this way
you have reached me
though you are so far

Thunder Stone- Chapter of Pining

Eagle Soldier's poem

I am done for
seeing this beauty you are
heard your lullaby
in a pebble
and caught your wild eyes
in the autumn maple
leaves
upon the loam
how
could I ever lean
or buckle
except to sink into the lichen
and feel you
where have you been
all this time
it's late
smoke rises
up

Harvest

And in this dream
i was that of a
cornfield
the men did come
and harvest the corn
a small girl came
she did make a doll
from this harvest
the doll did sit
and look to the west
there that harvest
doll did sit

Chapter 65- Which You Must Sail To

Near the lighthouse at Jonnie's
where the spilled blood makes sharks hungry
where some carefully dump their burdens
        into the sea
casting nets near the mouth
and the bay becomes a frenzy
all come to the orgy
seabirds dance on whitecaps
I too carry on like this in this cold
spinning my dog's hair into a fine thread
a cap for winter mixed with hag ribbons
which trail behind me like tails
Bohemian scarves tattered lace and
        knotted promises
waiting for the snap of big branches
hands calloused clearing the roads-
        shoveling mud moving granite
we like the cold. deep in our bones here
and move in our boots heavy as anchors—
        just an appearance
in the campfire the cove song crackles
brings on the North's front
and we stay—
chop wood

sharpen tools
bake bread
mend the road

Song from His Pebble

There are
wild things left
waft of smoke- a song
the earliest dove
still in the morning drift
verses snagged onto
that star the twirling leaf
upon the stream
hands that way
the visual the audible
talisman passed from one
to another so that
their own may always
find their way

Fervent Aperture

This
where the Red tail and Kite feed well
and the Owl's cough is intricate and varied
we step around it quietly still seeing
still hearing the field mice scurry within
ghost grasses burn ripe in this moon
locusts are on the grain
antlers lock somewhere in the night close by
causing a great ruckus on the earth
the stronger of the two pushed the other
across the scrub brush to the base
of Fist Mountain
which took a long time
seemingly

we grow still inside quiet listening and
find peace in the disorder the rattling and
grind the push and shove They leave their
tracks for those
who honor such battles
a small stone shows itself there in the
dusty furrows inside it a bear thunder
we pause listening again perhaps we keep it
or let it go to another
who may need it more
we ourselves are only the smallest

green in malachite
our faces fading on the bark and rocks
of deep orange lichen
marrow of sustenance cool pine needles
beneath bare feet
see us in the feather strike of the flame
the pine seed winged strange butterflies
cupped hands
we are river
reaching salt
buffalo against
alien wire Goodbye
we are the Black Salmon sucking we defy
often dying close to each other
pit our breastbone to the moons
lightning has struck water and rock
The Great Wind has swept it
we are ready

Chapter 68- Many Worlds

The brackish water
a sister to the desert
I won't say why   but you know that reason

you are my sky   a constellation of wild
          horses   windturned
I see you in twilight
you a blue sail moving west   together
          we were are
moonflowers   luminous
the hours after midnight see us

he said
"Man is put in his place on the pacific coast"

morning
you are meadowlark
sliver of light through the solstice
i bend down under the somniferum
drink you from that spring

she said
"Votif desire
  votif flame
   a candle"

i see you
emeralds in between the mountain

Chapter of Navigation and Loss

We're here beneath the furled leaf I try to
cover myself. A small marching dreaming
singing. I know your skeleton closet and
the bottom/end of things. I see you in your
manner. I fall into your winter. This snowrain
is making tiny lakes here here and here but the
water is different now. I too am frozen tonight.
I skip wishing rocks into the River Styx and
am always reaching back to Snakeback Ridge.
It is February. Season of remembering and
dismissal, a time to walk out of the room,
get on a plane to meet a lover thousands
of miles. lifetimes twilight. It's tender now
after all these years. I forget my own tongue
waste the money only to come back home
alone. I remember everyone everything and
everywhere so I take handfuls of Xanax and
smoke hashish drink spiked coffee refusing
to answer the phone wrote my Will instead
reword the Advance Directive. Heave my life
into the hefty bag leave it on the street. Again.
A real piece of work I say to myself about
myself. It is my private season of thunder.
Tonight I am chewing lichen cypress and blue

grass lilies lining up tiny bottles of bayou water broken glass and coins from the border towns. These are the coordinates back to the people who loved me more than I could bear.

Chapter 71- Owner of White, Red, and Black Horses

flowering vine
Passiflora incarnata coils beneath
the iron pergola   Still beautiful
when no one sees
my mouth made me an orphan
when i was 9
my words telling how her new man
tried to fuck me
so I shot him   She never forgave me
stringy haired girl
enemy of the camp
who owns the saber
someday you too will walk out
of all your chapters   And arrive in the far-off
copper leaf skin   Wing fragments your shawl
sipping dew from the Lady's Mantle
pilgrimage of thunder

Dark Magic

Crescent moon. Coyotes play
in the back pasture throwing their voices
wherever they want. I know better than to
believe them. Laying on my back in the dry
grass a star filled sky. I remember that last
time she was here. How I stayed away 'til she
passed out with her rum. Sometimes I have to
work dark magic.

gourd remains hidden
last winter we were friends
by July not so

6X2 Rattle

I am sure
was too drunk to notice how wonderful you
were
I sat humming
Or drumming
In between the bell pattern and
rattle's 6×2-rhythm
Somebody skin me
And excuse me
While I vomit
My last five
Exits out of society
Give me grace
Forgive my absence
And confusion
For what is human
And what is it to love?
13 It is the hour Of vertigo
And flickering light
That makes you question
Your eyesight   Again
Cataract perhaps like the moon
at times Slowly dimming
Softening the world
Fear

Is a small mountain
Which below
Is a vast and endless root system
Of the Four Earth Gods
Which In prayer
You know to be One
Screaming child
The white snow
Bleeds its cold hand
Around the sumac suckers
North Wind commands
Us into next season
Put your head to the Ground

Nadziitsa

sidewinders draw out maps
in the sand   Using their spine and sorrow
here is your chaparral Unsurprisingly
a sister to fire

Bay Chapter- To Heal

i float on the sea and am laria

I want you to know how to do this

how to lay in the tub with the bay leaves

Until your pain disappears

Shapeshifting- The Dark Chapter

i dropped to the ground last night
became an ocelot
saw you in your manner
blue of night echoed
became a shooting star
clay women mud woman who left everything
to find you
regret seeps in
sour honey in my mouth
once beatitude
became the hard flower

Murder Mountain, Alderpoint

morning

emeralds on our pulse points line a trail to
creation
we are smoke beneath the sequoia
kaleidoscope vision
though the leaf of a madrone
the ins and outs of the universe

spring summer

sun shafts of light
pour down to the
jeweled path of trillium ovatum usnea
morning initiates the queen
sex dirt and honey under our nails
honest work for the most part

night

autumn fog descends
over the years became our skin
crowned our dreams
where we
forever long for her

sometimes grieving
sunset though the rattle grass

autumn winter

dragged across the sky by
October's moon
too tired to move even a finger
anointed and held by
the true scent of fire
here we are redwood and mycelium
arc of the rose hips a portal
we cry in February
back against the mountain floor
frozen grass crunching
under our dreams
wild

Chapter 78- True Medicine

She cat moves
like liquid over the desert
and is the gold and copper
of the sacred clown's vision
nocturnal she stays awake
marauder of the Mojave
dining on jackrabbit and fox
she knows the secret stairway
to the top of black mesa
and how to survive
the journey out of the gutter
dream to her through the
night blooming Ceruse
true vanilla and sugar
of the desert
medicine for grief
and the great went

Chapter 79- Own Magic

You know your own magic What it can do
i want to say cruel but it's not
to remind me of myself
what I once was am still
how I know
your tongue in my mouth
vetiver and ylang ylang
blossom under our grasp
becomes our skin our walk
i look for you under the forsythia

Chapter 80- California

waning summer
she sleeps
in a season of new lovers
found too late as we board planes
and other realities
cannabis and driftwood smoke
sea foam combined with the cinnamon of sex
you know you're in California
garlic coffee and buckeye
a song in the late afternoon

Chapter 81- Togethering

the forked lightning goes to sleep
softly For a season or lifetime
long after butterflies become swallows
then starlings
We come together and part like that
animal sad
you bring your wounds
to the bold prairie that is somehow
the sea and sky at once
we've set down our sorrows
and now i lay with hips wide open to the stars
i have become the cobalt sky
how is it that we missed our togethering
you are this openness The sea too far from me
reach reaching. I know us together
stars and petal storms All this twilight

Chapter 82- The Edgewitch

she's in the woods
perhaps you know her
she lives on the edges
of things and places
eats with her hands
follows the shadows
dragging her mud boots
through the usnea and cedar
through tomorrow and lasterday
smells like rainwater tastes of copper
faces on the redwoods
crushed eggshells underfoot
where we put things to rest
unbind it from our seventh direction
this is how we vow
make our own prayer
this is where we make pacts
to clouds mountains autumn vineyards
to be better for one another
the past sometimes hurts
leave it
war in the rooms
meat on the table
this is what men are made of
what you're made of

and the sea that too
granite and the flood tide
I know you this way
Northwind
a hard lesson
cypress scraping the sky
cigars and good rum
loving fast
loving completely
loving deeply
tangled
falling asleep on haiku

True Weight of the Sea

arrowleaf balsam root
pearl everlasting
this is North and East of here
laminaria
sea palm fronds
bladderwrack
marker 47- Salt Point
where we learned the true weight of the sea
beneath the dead pine
20 pounds of boletes
2 many husbands
the dumb sky/see how it hangs
25 years later
drop off regrets at the station
glow
a new day
awesome blossom
20 blankets is my home
/remember the tule elk at Manka's/
fog

We Speak of Mighty Things

here on Mount Vision I trace your face
a crescent moon above the Monterey cypress
and long to speak to you
of the phosphorescence in the hidden cove
i want to ask you do you remember?
if not I will tell you this

late well after midnight the eucalyptus
    bent down so deeply she reached
        into the sea touched it
this was the season of fury
a time when artists tear their studios apart
cuss God and break their most precious
        possessions in one night
season of secrets and making pacts
we eat stale bread drink rum
and walk through the opium after midnight
          evermore
              driftwood smoke
                        here i will always know you

we are out at Laird's Landing
and slipped out of our clothes and
        into the sea
swimming under the full moon

We are Illuminated
and became a school of perch
then 7000 swallows
i try to retrace the steps and spy a glance
of the she-cat
she must have left when you did

Savage Woman- Chapter of Starbursts

tell your woman I don't care
let her know I'm mad and aloof
with tangled hair
a monster who bites at your trapezius
as you enter me Blinds you and covers
your ears at orgasm
how you see starbursts and 10,000 years
of indigo blowing in the wind in your ecstasy
tell her of the shared visions Wolves
running through Broken Doll Pass
and bald eagles Locking talons in a death
spiral How you'll never give up
this medicine and that I told you you belong
to no one and all your
Relations at once Tell her I know
what true freedom is and that
I skip stones across the River Styx

Chapter 86- Eternal

you
ambergris beneath my navel
you the sea
primordial heat in the loam
source of the sugar on my astral body
come to me always
this vertigo Kiss me bourbon and vanilla
time is short Meet me beneath the dead pine
belly to earth We discover ourselves Eternal

Chapter 87- Directions to The Night She Got Free

(or, the night she escaped her captors- the Deer Hunter and Gunsmith)

Get your gear in order:

the whetting stones for the carbon steel knives

a good lock for the door

Guinness and Valium

Camels hardbox unfiltered

your bulletproof vest

made from passiflora incarnata and

blue ribbon beer tabs from 1974

a shell casing rattle

your iron boots

the will to live

you must be fluent in the language of alcohol
poisoning and black out drunk
a way to reach the unhinged realm
she's gone again

Pack your truck for a solo trip

strap it down using a trucker's hitch and a
pocketful of hopefuls

head west and north you will have to walk
through the vineyards

at night during harvest time

month of fire season of excess indulgence

evacuation and disorientation

lay on the ground Right before dawn make
your way down the ridge

to wash your hair using dew you collect from
the Lady's Mantle polish your crown
wear the red lipstick let your eyeliner run
weep with both palms on the ground
weep some more then get up stuff your
mouth using your two hands

with late season Muscat grapes. wild boar
sausages vagrancy and damask rose petals
let it all run down your arms let go of your
mind

those with a weak suck at birth should not
follow you here

tell them to not wait for you

don't follow don't follow don't follow
don't follow

" " " "

" " " *goodbye*

Leave town irresponsibly without a plan

pick up a topo map along the way and

follow the dragon veins along the east side of
the Sierras

ride the backbone of California

where men are put in their place Fall in love

Make a big plan   Make promises Fall out of
love

Give it all away
seek solitude   Soak in the hot springs then be
silent

and watch the sunset   Fall asleep singing

an invisibility song   complete with a flicker
feather

tied in your hair   Wake up in Joshua Tree and
sit in the dirt

get down on your belly and collect tiny
crystals

from the anthills just lay there

make a bundle with them chaparral and a
traveling song

then lineup 365 .45 caliber hollow points

count them and your blessings   then carefully

sew them into your inseam alongside Ativan

copal and peonia seeds

lean against huge boulders bigger

than all your collective regrets   Leave them there

sip mezcal from a demitasse as you walk out

into the Mojave with Owl's clover blossoms in your hair

Song During Worm Moon

We are eating meat raw
close to the bone in everyplace
where reservations   villages   alleyways
        and barrios
are desperate and haggard   Grandmas
        set down their Nescafé
pinching off the dead leaves in their dim and
        congested rooms
they have ceased waiting for the letters
        to come   The phone to ring

go ahead husband
here is your soup
                altar
        smoke
cupful of seashells
    turned to sand

my back arched just for you
swan neck illusionist
golden throat hummingbird
your pit viper

drink this
your holy water

you are the only king here
see the way
you search for my hips at night
slipping your hands in between my thighs
        to warm them
                                they are cold

and not just from winter
you're a mean bastard but that doesn't
        move me
you know where comfort is

stringent bite of the bitterroot escapes from
my mouth   it's what I do

"You're too strong," you say
but you really wouldn't have it
any other way

"... nation is not conquered until
the hearts of its women are on the ground. ...

you fall asleep
your knees feet and past vagrancies

then it is done, no matter how brave
it's warriors,
nor how strong their weapons."

heavy upon me
i heave you over and off me
easily as one of the children
while singing a protection song

you do not stir
this house smells like onion bread and liver
you sleep easy that way

Chapter of Grief-
Owner of Hag Ribbons

redbud blooms

unshy as you grieve

vermillion

mockingbird

there's no one left at noontide

Chapter 90- Where You Pack Your Truck

she

left

at twilight

goodbye love

when raptors take flight

there is a small hope on the road

here

she

exhales

atropa

consort of spirits

she's better up in the mountains

Chapter 91- Mourning Ground (Bloody Bay, Tobago West Indies 1996)

be there

shanty roads

Charlotteville fêtes on Saturdays

pink blue purple houses

dressed in pelou and black cake

bottle tree prayers

and the sting of bird pepper

in the Horse's eye

the Mourning Ground has gone awry

pan man somewhere practicing for next week

i hear this in between the bell rhythm

buried

i am in my grave

a 6/8 bell pattern

a Mother's church bell

a boy and his staff

Bacongo, DRC

blind and deaf

am i here or here?

who battles inside the House?

the white of the eye sees this

what has happened

what will come to pass

draw it out on the sea-grape leaves

here is your chalk

only

where are you now?

some ask

to and fro

to and fro

jumping banana boats toward a home

we are red orphans so tiny in the sea

we loved though imperfect

Blue Water Boy

pinion
juniper
our cousin- copal
the bead between my teeth

we are smoke on the dried river
tins cans there now
huff town u.s.a
a shame
a hidden something
tossed warrior

a go away girl
a not so long girl
a there not there girl

interstate 8 drives us straight into the pacific
118° delirious heat
our hair is on fire in my old Ford pickup
saguaro cactus Grandfather
can i stay?
sleep in your purple world
do i have to go?

juniper carrying boy

blue water boy
smiling too much boy
comes along for the ride
to fall in
to fall out of love

be the jackrabbit
be the small fox
your corn pollen
has washed away the shadow ones
i am sure of it

feel Good
feel God

Holy Bayou

He fashioned her from the jut
Of the Cypress knee
Of a strange Medicine did he mold her
But arthritic like her mother's
Silhouette She was not
Only ancient and green
As the Spanish moss
Heavy with it

Powder of the white shell
Powder you safe with it
Mark of the innocent
Mask of the Holy
May your head be cool
First Medicine

Scatter
With the egret
And they turn to tend their young
Scatter
Into the sun and warmth

Leave it
To those

Swamp natured ones
chicca-chicca-chicca
"The cottonmouth
And alligator are
My Brothers"

Belly of the coons
Screech owl
Water moccasins
Welcome her
Pole to the bayou
Hyacinth moving
And it leaves no tracks

Powder of the cascarilla
Dust you safe
with it
Womb of the
Bayou
Shoot of the falling star
and two eyes ease out
shining
then descend
Her Brothers in
The night
pole into Holy Bayou
push on
push on

pirogue deep into the
Manchac

Ashton Tallghost Appeals to St. Barbara, St. Theresa Saint. James, Trinidad, West Indies

a fist
a heart
a jeweled yam
the black aubergine offering

Here is my battle axe

your dreams run into hers
mouth moving so fast
yet like an unusual water Loa
you dredge through the swamps
hardly lifting your feet
arms paralyzed
unable to rise
it is the million-mile night

"You will be uprooted if you leave,"
Belle had said, but still you went

the Batas
1,2,3 from them countryras in Saint George
you have been cursed for whoring them

and are now pleading

"Wrap me in the flags
Palm oil and rum
6
333
9
float me in the bowl with the marigolds
        and blue

St. Barbara help me
St. Theresa go easy
St. Barbara help me,"

delirious
you see patterns though the mosquito net
that bodie is climbing the walls,
        Spanish thyme
pressing into your pillow, bakers dust
        on your palms

"Here is a coffee, and some biscuits
        for ya Star,"

painting the iron bed yellow then green
the new coverlet
it is never clean enough
sleeping with the fan

cooking dog food
walking that hill

"St. Barbara
St. Barbara
Who Rules This Place
I am choking on your thunderbolt,"

and when you awaken
you move like a dead man

he is mad they say
a conju on his head

they see you feed it by the three way
1
2
3
a new plate
it is Wednesday

Rest Easy Under the Dead Pine-
Chapter of Heathens

there is no map
to that place
of big sun and cut shadows

follow the edge of the palmate leaf
i am the red ant carrying

here where God and his eye
the heat Lightning

where
in my rage
a second… just

i was
became The nonbeliever

Strange breed II- Fern born

that Mississippi ride/claw
of that Choctaw's grip
her medicine had him whipped

arched and bent
like her cypress
pole to the water

ease into the saw
of the whine of the fiddle

blues harp tangled to the
tap and jingle
powdered sleep

flash of the thunder into Red Bayou
High John sits at the top of the temple

Cage Bloom

This is for you
Who has been gone a long time
Your whereabouts and what you did
        are unimportant

Me
I have been here
Within but not hidden among the Fern and
        Redwoods

How I love you in a way beyond distance

Boy of Sunshine
Boy of our Barrio
Boy of our Flatlands Deep Sticks and
        Cold Rivers
Boy at the Mouth of the Bay
You are the Black Salmon Running
Some whisper and say you will not make it
I know you will

Eye of laughter
Eye of many miles
Misunderstood
Boy of Good Heart

Who became a Man

You loved me in Rain Time you loved me
in Sun Time
For this   I will always remember

Black Sparrow

in heated chaos

in brightest clarity

winter's fold

black sparrow

split the sky

you are

the long shadow man

come   Come close

let us whisper this

passion

flood tide

you possess

Eye of the sky painter

silent

suave lover

red the mezcal

quick as the beaded whip

invisible

your medicine is strong

it tops the rattle

we are

slave and free

our open mouths bring the smell of rain

i cannot   cannot

can

reach the clouds and touch you

ride this

in translation this gets lost

leave it

we make love in this way

and sing a song we have never sung before

then are silent with the moon

strange leaves falling

scent the night floor

Aimé- Rue Royale by way of Pointe-Noire

1

Yes I know you from the
Shadows of Mekambo
And the small smell of
Palm oil rubbed into the masks

Yet my khush balm leaves you
Copper mouthed tumult of
Sensations Thunder Side of the Camp

2

Cleaning out the fountain
In the courtyard of that place
We had on Rue Royale

Water lilies and papyrus had
Overtook it and I tore the roots apart
Lifting out the magnolia petals that
Fell in summer dipping in the still water

Where your bone wishes had coiled
And cleaved to it's coolness in the humidity

While everyone in the Quarter slept
Behind the filigree wrought iron like the
Dead in the oldest of the Parishes

3

Top Hat called from Blood River
Rounding up the animals and galvanize

But there was too much vagrancy
In your promises and dreams
And you failed to be the great
Voyant sad solider broken cart

Yet
Not everyone knew how the Great
Bamboo cut like razor blades
No one can take that from you
In this way you were somehow
Pardoned

4

Down the street with chicory
And beignets your laughter lagged
With Tucker and Brossard
When my slightest glance

Unfrocked you

O how you longed for the
Cicada and Dutch Wax
And knew secretly why the
Blacksmiths are so special

Lucky Bastard

They all knew I was born
Of thunder
And a river that splits
In two
And knew too
That the arch
Of my brow
Could send them cottonwoods asway
Hearts*
That's what the child
In me named them
And they shake
In the moon of my birth
Lucky Bastard
My Sweet Love knows me
Lucky Bastard
I know him too
A sailor's mouth
From my father
My mother of mudstone and shale
So I shrug at the plates colliding
And ride the mountain
Without fear
Lucky Bastards
My sweet love knows me

Lucky Bastard
I know him too

* *Populus deltoides*

Land like a Feather

Redwood lady
My veil above me lady
Hush and hush
Our whispering lady

All around me is Thunder
Coyote I love you
I see you looking away
I do not see you
This is the way

Seeing

Manzanita Madrone
Capture fire in your branches
Sweep the trail
Clean over the Moon

Stone I am beneath you

Untitled

Deer fern
Oshala
High Sierra Valerian
I am the feral and uncultivated
Petal
Leaf
Oxalis for a parched world
I have become the poison root so bitter
I have become the sweet root
Rising
I come to the end of things
Secrecy sees me
I bless
I curse

Chapter 103- Becoming Rattlegrass

it's easy for me to stop loving you
The way the bobcat becomes rattlegrass
        on Inverness ridge
The way a footprint is the mainsail
        then the lost visa   You're not new
I'm datura along I-5   A ghost rattle   This is
        how i came to Bloody Bay Tobago
and to a husband who made sure the
        cupboard was full
but dragged me by my hair
from the bed to the joining room
        This is how women become
        fog and smoke
and
1000 starlings   leaving the city
        before you awaken

Waxing Crescent- Chapter of Power

sorcerers always find her
usually in secret Always in secret
complicated men with more passion
than their worlds can understand
they look too closely and know women
        too well
have traced their collarbones
        to flowered valleys
their tongues follow the hitch of her hip
and know too well how to hurt and love them
men that are wind   Men that are rain
        in February
Men like that a herd of horses at
        Pryor Mountain
taste like dirt and cypress from the coast
Men like that keep their secrets safe
How they planned then didn't
        follow through
destroying their own selves with
        their pills and
powders and room temperature liqueur
bloody knuckles Just you and the wall
a 38 wrapped in an old Pendleton scrap
there's always that
don't get me wrong i'm not a savior

just a woman
you and i
we stay up all night arranging peonies and
        winged seeds
Never far from one another on all shores
        it is the same

hammering copper into the walls
Storms of violets and vodka
don't cry lover
a grief welling up flying towards the
moonglade
the wood thrush questioning you
you are my sea

Summer Chant

Sunrise

Lady's Mantle it's been a long time
since i've seen you
Dew Holder
Early One
thank you for this vision
thank you for this medicine

Midnight

i can't tell you how it is here
how it even showed itself
but it folds the sky
is the creation of sugar in the forest
night smoke
screech owl
tonight i line up 7 gourds
set them under the red bud
water
gold dust
four bar cross fashioned from the manzanita
a thin long string a trap really
to be followed
berries strung through linen

Holy door and Watcher
thank you for showing yourself here
thank you for the song
thank you for
clarity of vision
clarity of dream
precision of my arrow
my ability to fly

ABOUT THE AUTHOR

Jolaoso Prettythunder lives in the deep woods of Northern California on the native land and home of the Kashaya Pomo, with her family and two dogs, Rosie Farstar and Ilumina Holy Dog. She is a farmer, freedom grower, practitioner and student of herbal medicine and the founder of The Cloud Women's Dream Society, as well as a contributor and publisher of Cloud Women's Quarterly Journal. She is a well-traveled poet who loves rock, porch swings, pickup trucks, cooking, campfires, lightning, steak, long drives, hot cups of coffee, gathering and making medicine and singing with friends and family. She is a practitioner of Indigenous Spiritual and healing traditions.

www.ingramcontent.com/pod-product-compliance
Lightning Source LLC
Chambersburg PA
CBHW051110160426
43196CB00029B/2588
* 9 7 8 1 8 8 9 5 6 8 1 7 1 *